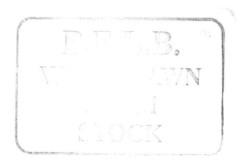

PIONEERS IN HISTORY
THINKERS

MICHAEL POLLARD

HEINEMANN CHILDREN'S REFERENCE
a division of Heinemann Educational Books Ltd
Halley Court, Jordan Hill, Oxford OX2 8EJ

OXFORD LONDON EDINBURGH
MELBOURNE SYDNEY AUCKLAND
MADRID ATHENS BOLOGNA
SINGAPORE IBADAN NAIROBI HARARE
GABORONE KINGSTON PORTSMOUTH NH(USA)

ISBN 0 431 00554 0

British Library Cataloguing in Publication Data
Pollard, Michael, 1931–
    Thinkers.
    1. Intellectuals - Biographies - Collections
    I. Title   II. Series
305.5′52′0922

© Heinemann Educational Books Ltd 1991
First published 1991

Designed by Pardoe Blacker Limited
Picture research by Faith Perkins
Maps by Kevin Diaper

Printed in Hong Kong

90 91 92 93 94 95 10 9 8 7 6 5 4 3 2 1

Photographic credits

a = above b = below r = right l = left

The author and publishers wish to acknowledge, with
thanks, the following photographic sources:

The cover pictures are courtesy of The Bridgeman Art
Library and Peter Newark's Historical Pictures

Bettmann Archive pp30, 32; Bridgeman Art Library pp title
page, 4, (Vatican Museums & Galleries), 11a (Duomo,
Florence), 12 (British Library), 14a, 15, 18 (Giraudon), 19b,
21a, 22 (Labour Society), 26, 27a; British Library p7b; Mary
Evans Picture Library pp11b, 16, 24b; Giraudon/Lauros 19a;
Ronald Grant Archive p35a; Hulton-Deutsch Collection
pp12a, 23b, 24a, 38, 39a, 41a; Sonia Halliday Photographs
pp6, 7a, 9a; IDAF p42; Magnum pp15 (Chris Steele
Perkins); Peter Newark's Pictures pp13a and b, 17b, 20, 23a,
25, 27b, 28, 29a, 31, 33l and r, 36; George Orwell Archive,
University College, London p35b; Popperfoto pp34, 37a
and b, 40; Ann Ronan p29b; Scala pp9b, 10 (Uffizi), 14b;
Topham Picture Library pp41b, 43b.

The publishers have made every effort to trace the copyright
holders, but if they have inadvertently overlooked any,
they will be pleased to make the necessary arrangements at
the first opportunity.

Note to the reader
In this book there are some words in the text which are printed in **bold** type. This shows that the word is
listed in the glossary on page 46. The glossary gives a brief explanation of words which may be new to you.

Contents

Introduction

People have always asked themselves questions about where they came from and what life was for. The first people who lived on Earth left records of their lives by painting hunting scenes on cave walls, but we do not know what they thought. It is difficult to convey a thought in a picture.

Eventually, the cave dwellers of pre-history developed ways of **communicating** with others. They did not use words at first but communicated by using sounds like animals. Over thousands of years, people learned to speak by using signs, then words or spoken language to describe their actions. Soon, they could tell stories to each other, pray to the gods and question them about the mysteries of life.

Words and ideas

Later, people found that language could be used to talk about ideas. If there were no words for new ideas, new words could be made up. People tried out ideas and started a **debate** by discussing their ideas with other people. In some early **civilizations**, such as those of Greece and Rome, debating schools were very popular. People would go along to hear well-known speakers take part.

▼ The Italian painter Raphael painted this fresco between 1508 and 1511. The central figures, Plato and Socrates, are surrounded by many of the famous philosophers from ancient times.

► Printing made it possible for more people to find out more about other people's ideas. In today's newspaper we can read about what people were saying and thinking yesterday.

Once there was a written language and ideas could be written down, more people could learn about them and they could be carried from one place to another. Before printing was invented in 1440, all books had to be written and copied by hand. This took a long time, and was of no use to people who could not read at all. Those who could read had more chance to find out about other people's ideas and discuss them.

How ideas spread

When books were first printed in Europe over 500 years ago, few people could afford to buy them. By about 150 years ago, the printing of books in huge quantities reduced the production costs considerably. Books could then be sold at a price that most people could afford. At the same time, more and more people were going to school and learning to read and write.

Ideas could be read and talked about by ordinary people, not just by great thinkers. Today, television, radio and the newspapers bring us new ideas every day, and we can all take part in discussing them.

This is the reason why new ideas spread more quickly now than in the past. The thinkers of ancient Greece were heard by only a small number of people, and their ideas spread slowly to others. Radio and television carry ideas quickly to millions of people all over the world.

Thinkers can change the way we look at ourselves and the world around us. They help us to make sense of our lives, but thinkers are not always welcome. Their ideas may conflict with those of the rulers of their countries or influential citizens. Many speakers and writers have been put in prison to stop them spreading their ideas. Some thinkers' writings or speeches have been taken away, or **banned**, to prevent others from reading or hearing them.

The ancient Greeks

Over 2000 years ago, Athens was one of the main cities of ancient Greece. It was a wealthy city, and its leading citizens had time to increase their understanding and knowledge of the world. They were the first people to study **philosophy**, the understanding of ideas. Some philosophers wrote stories and plays which included their ideas about right and wrong doings. This made the ideas easier to understand and meant that they could be discussed by a greater number of people.

One of the first of the Greek philosophers was Socrates, who was born in 469 BC. He liked to spend his time in the market place of Athens where he met and talked with all sorts of people, especially the young. Socrates believed that people should work out why they thought as they did. So he encouraged others to ask themselves questions about their beliefs, such as: What is courage? What is just or fair? What is self-control? This search for the truth angered some of the leaders of Athens, and at the age of about 70 Socrates was condemned to death.

Socrates believed it was better to suffer wrong-doing then to escape punishment. He could have escaped from prison but he refused and died by drinking poisonous hemlock.

► Socrates lived in Greece over 2000 years ago and was one of history's most important thinkers. A modest man, Socrates did not claim to be wise or to possess any knowledge about the world but he spent all his life teaching others how to learn more about themselves.

Plato, learner and teacher

The ideas of Socrates were followed by younger men, such as Plato who also lived in Athens. Plato was 30 when Socrates died. He was interested in the way government worked, and he was the first person to think deeply about **politics**, the art of government.

Plato wrote over 30 books. The most famous, *The Republic*, is still read by students of politics and philosophy today. In this book, Plato describes a system of

▲ The agora, the market place of Athens, was the favourite meeting place of the philosophers. There they could debate their ideas with other citizens. Part of the agora, the stoa, has been rebuilt from the ruins of other buildings.

government called a **republic** in which power is held by the people, not by one ruler alone. Plato's friend, Socrates, did not leave any writings but Plato wrote down the debates he imagined Socrates might have had with his friends. This illustrated Socrates's method of asking questions and debating the answers.

Plato was an important teacher as well as a writer. When he was about 40 years old, he started a school in Athens where he taught younger men about his ideas. This school was called the Academy, and it was the world's first university where young people came to learn and debate. Plato lived to the age of 80, but the Academy continued after his death for another 800 years.

Aristotle

Aristotle was one of Plato's students. He went to the Academy when he was 17 and studied there for 20 years. He left Athens when Plato died in 347 BC but returned when he was nearly 50 to set up his own school called the Lyceum. He wrote about a wide range of subjects covering the world of nature, human life and history. Science was his main interest and he was the first thinker to split science up into its separate parts, such as the study of animals, **biology**, and the study of the stars, **astronomy**.

Although some of his scientific ideas were wrong, Aristotle was especially good at researching and gathering facts. He laid down many rules that scientists still follow today. One of these rules was the grouping of things that are similar in appearance or in the way they behave. When scientists talk about a family group or species of animals or plants, they are using one of Aristotle's ideas.

▼ Aristotle teaching philosophy to the Emperor Alexander when he was a child.

St Thomas Aquinas

Long after Aristotle died in 322 BC, thinkers in Europe continued to argue about his ideas. After a lifetime of careful thought and research, Aristotle had based his ideas on **reason**. About 400 years after his death, the teaching of the Christian Church began to play an important part in people's lives and thoughts. Christians believed that they should follow Christ's teaching without question. This kind of belief is called faith.

For hundreds of years, it looked as if there would always be a clash between the people who reasoned like Aristotle and the faithful Christians. As the Church became more established, universities were built where Christian ideas were studied. This study is called **theology**. Many Church leaders believed that Aristotle's ideas should be forgotten.

Reason and faith

In 1239, a 15-year-old prince arrived in Naples in Italy to study at the university. His name was Thomas Aquinas. Soon afterwards, he joined a group of monks called the Dominicans, who spent their lives preaching. Thomas Aquinas's family were so upset by this that they arranged for him to be kidnapped and held prisoner, but after a few months he was allowed to return to the university. From then on he spent his life learning, teaching and writing in the universities of Europe in Paris, Cologne, Rome and Naples.

Thomas Aquinas believed that all ideas, Aristotle's as well as Christian, came from God. He wrote several books comparing the two sets of ideas and showing how they fitted together. In 1265 he started on

◀ Centres of learning and teaching were established around monasteries and cathedrals and became known as universities.

his answers. The questions were ones that worried Christians at the time, such as what God is like and what it means to say that God is good. Thomas Aquinas was still writing his major book when he died in 1274, and it was finished by one of his students.

▲ Thomas Aquinas was a large man who preferred quiet discussion to fierce argument. As a student, his quietness earned him the nickname of 'the dumb ox', but he was listening and learning all the time.

his most important book of all, called *The Sum of Theology*. He wrote that people could reason out many ideas for themselves, as Aristotle did. Other ideas could be known only by people who had faith in God.

In *The Sum of Theology* Thomas asked over 500 questions, to which he then gave

Thomas and the Church

Many leaders of the Church did not want their own ideas questioned, and disagreed with Thomas Aquinas. They were afraid that if people were encouraged to think for themselves they might begin to ask questions about the Church and its leaders. Thomas Aquinas did not waste time arguing, but went on steadily with his work to the day he died.

Fifty years after Thomas's death, the Pope added his name to the list of saints. However, it was to be another 500 years before Pope Leo XIII ordered that Thomas's books should be studied by all student priests of the Catholic Church. Today Thomas Aquinas's books are still read by people who want to understand how Church teaching fits in with the ideas of the Greek thinkers.

▼ A typical university classroom in the Middle Ages.

Dante Alighieri

Dante Alighieri was born in Italy in 1265. When he was about nine, something happened to Dante which changed his life. He met a girl of the same age, Beatrice, and fell in love with her. Beatrice grew up, married and died at the age of about 25 without knowing about this, but Dante went on loving her for the rest of his life. As he grew older, he thought of Beatrice as a kind of saint who would lead him to heaven.

As a young man, Dante became one of the leaders of Florence. It was at a time when groups of people were struggling to rule the city and its wealth. There were several clashes over the years but in 1302 Dante failed to make peace between two groups and three days of street fighting followed. As a result Dante and others were forced to leave the city in order to escape the threat of death by burning. He had to leave his wife and children behind and was never able to return. The rest of his life was spent in **exile**, travelling from place to place and staying with friends.

Dante's journey

About the time he left Florence, Dante began writing his most famous book, *The Divine Comedy*. It is a long poem which tells the story of how he is lost in a dark forest and kept prisoner there by wild animals. A guide comes to rescue him and lead him on a journey.

Everything that happens in the story has a meaning. The dark forest is Dante's idea of life, with all its worries and troubles. The guide who leads him out of it is knowledge. On his journey, Dante meets famous people from history and also many people he knew during his life. Some of them are suffering terrible punishments because of the wrong they did during their lives.

◀ A wall painting, or fresco, of Dante Alighieri.

► This painting of part of *The Divine Comedy* shows Dante standing in front of the mountain of Purgatory. People who have done wrong have to climb the mountain to reach heaven.

Heaven at last

At the end of Dante's book, after many adventures, he reaches heaven. There, he finds Beatrice waiting for him. She guides him around heaven, and at the end of his journey he understands everything about the meaning of life and death.

If Dante had simply written down his ideas, they would have been read only by **scholars**. Like Greek plays which were written for a wide audience, stories could be enjoyed by more readers. Dante also made his book easier to read by writing it in the Italian language. At that time, most books were still written in Latin, which most people could not read. *The Divine Comedy* showed how, in Dante's mind, knowledge, religion and everyday life were all linked together.

Dante was an important poet whose ideas were taken up during his life by writers and artists from France, England and Germany. Today, *The Divine Comedy* gives readers an idea of how Europeans lived and thought nearly 700 years ago.

► On his journey, Dante passes through hell and sees the sufferings of people whose lives have been wicked. With him, on the left, is the Roman poet Virgil, his guide to knowledge.

Desiderius Erasmus

By 1500, the Catholic Church had become the most important power in Europe. The Pope as leader of the Church, was more powerful than any king. The Church owned all the schools and universities and could stop the spread of new ideas.

The Church was wealthy, and many of its bishops and priests had become lazy. They collected taxes from the people and spent it on palaces for the Pope and his bishops. Greed and rich living had taken the place of the old belief of caring for the poor. Some priests thought that changes were needed and Desiderius Erasmus was among them.

▼ The four bishops, in white pointed hats on the right, are having a meal with the King of Portugal. Bishops enjoyed fine clothes and good food while ordinary people had to struggle to live.

Laughing at the Church

Erasmus was educated by monks, but disliked and disbelieved much of what he was taught. It seemed to him that Church teaching had little to do with the lives of ordinary people, or with the beliefs of the early Christians, such as Saint Peter and Saint Paul.

When Erasmus was 23, he went to the University of Paris. Afterwards wealthy friends and patrons helped him to travel throughout western Europe in England and Italy. He looked for teaching work wherever he could.

Meanwhile, he had begun to write about his ideas for change in the Church. Erasmus's way of attacking the leaders of the Church was to make fun of them. This kind of writing is called **satire**. In 1509, he

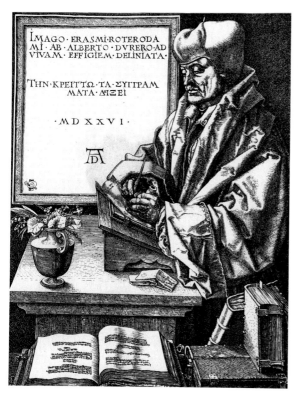

▲ An engraving of Erasmus writing at his desk, at the age of about 60.

and early Christians, but it was written in Greek which meant that few people could understand it. Erasmus translated the *New Testament* into Latin so that educated people could see the difference between what the *New Testament* really said and what the Church taught.

After Erasmus

Erasmus's writing got him into trouble with the Church, which banned his books to try to stop people reading them. He had shown for the first time that it was possible to ask questions about the church and even laugh at it. Towards the end of his life, his ideas began to lead to the Reformation, a religious movement which split the Christian Church in two. The Catholic Church continued with the Pope as its head, but the **Protestant** churches led by the religious reformer Martin Luther broke away from the Catholics. Erasmus was caught between the two sides. He had started to make important changes but he could not stop the violence that followed. He was saddened by the smashing of religious images and loss of order in the Church. Yet until Erasmus died in 1536, he continued to preach a gospel of reason and Christian charity.

wrote a book called *In Praise of Folly*. In it, he pretended to praise foolish people, such as monks who cared more about the way they dressed than about teaching the Christian gospel. People enjoyed laughing at the foolishness of some people in the Church, but they also understood Erasmus's message that things must change. As books were now printed in Germany, Italy and England, Erasmus's book could now reach a large number of readers.

Soon after the book was published, Erasmus began a larger and more difficult task. He knew that the Latin Bible used by the Church had many mistakes in it. Erasmus decided to correct these mistakes. The *New Testament* told the story of Christ

◀ The first printed books appeared in Germany around 1440. Although the first printing presses were slow, the process was much faster than copying the books by hand.

Galileo Galilei

It is difficult today to imagine a world in which there was hardly any knowledge of science, but until about 400 years ago this was true. People still accepted the ideas of Aristotle who had lived 2000 years before. The church had made Aristotle's ideas fit into religious thinking and did not want any changes. Many of those ideas were wrong, but few people questioned them.

Aristotle believed that the Earth was the centre of the solar system and that the Sun and planets revolved around it. In the early 1500s, a scientist named Nicholas Copernicus had the idea that the Sun, not the Earth, was the centre of the solar system. He had no proper means of studying the sky at night and so he could not prove his idea was correct.

▲ Galileo Galilei was the first person to see mountains and craters on the Moon through a telescope. He also worked on the branch of science which is now called physics. He carried out many experiments to find out, for instance, whether different weights did fall at different speeds.

▶ This is a model of Galileo's telescope. His work excited scientists all over Europe, and he made hundreds of telescopes so that they could share in his discoveries.

The telescope

In 1564, about 20 years after Copernicus's death, Galileo Galilei was born in Pisa in Italy. He began to study to be a doctor, but he found science more interesting. He liked asking himself questions about science and then searching for the answers just as Socrates had done. Galileo did not accept ideas unless he had carried out experiments which proved them for himself. One of the ideas he questioned was about the solar system.

In 1608, a Dutch scientist invented the telescope. This instrument enabled him to study the sky at night. Galileo heard about this and built a telescope of his own. Looking through it at night, he saw stars and planets that no one had ever seen before. By studying their movements, he discovered that Copernicus was right. The Earth and the other planets moved around the Sun.

Banned by the Pope

Other scientists were excited by Galileo's work, but the Pope ordered him to stop his experiments because his ideas on the Universe did not agree with the Church's teachings. Sadly, Galileo had to accept the Pope's orders, and he retired from university work. He went on working on his own, and in 1632, he published a book in support of the Copernicus theory. The Pope ordered that the book should not be sold, and Galileo was told to go to Rome to be tried by a Church court, the **Inquisition**, for refusing to accept the Church's teaching.

By this time, Galileo was old and ill, but

▲ This nineteenth-century painting shows Galileo facing the Inquisition in Rome in 1623. He was forced to deny that his findings about the solar system were true.

he was threatened with torture unless he denied that what he had written was true. He had no choice but to do as he was told, and after a few months in prison he was allowed to go free. He lived for another nine years and went on working until his death in 1642.

Galileo wrote many books on mechanics and did experiments on the laws of moving objects. Until Galileo's time, experiments only showed how things happened, not why. Education was based on reasoning rather than experiment. Galileo's main contribution to science was to show scientists how to think and work. He taught them that it was not enough simply to have an idea. Scientific ideas had to be tried out and proved by experiment. Gailieo's way of looking at scientific problems is one that scientists still use today.

John Milton

The invention of printing worried rulers, governments and the churches. It meant that new ideas could spread easily and quickly. They saw printing as a threat to their power. The English government was just as afraid of attacks on its power as any other. In 1637, a law was passed saying that books and papers must have a **licence** allowing them to be printed. Licences were given only if the government agreed with what the writers said.

Towards press freedom

John Milton was a poet and writer who thought that English people should be free to read or write what they liked. When he was 35 he married, but his wife Mary soon went home to her parents. He wrote a pamphlet, a short book, saying that the ending of a marriage by divorce should be allowed by law. This was a new and shocking idea. Milton knew that the

◄ John Milton was born a Catholic, but became a Protestant when he was a student. He joined the Puritans, a group of Protestants who believed in living and dressing plainly.

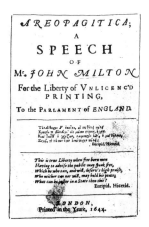

◀ The title page of Milton's *Areopagitica*. Although Milton wrote it like a speech which could have been read in Parliament, it was never read out in this way.

but in 1644 he wrote yet another pamphlet which he called *Areopagitica*. This was a more serious attack on government **censorship**. It demanded freedom for anyone to print anything they wished without a licence.

government would not agree with it, so he published his pamphlet without a licence.

As Milton expected, his pamphlet caused a great deal of anger in Parliament. Over the next two years, he published three more pamphlets arguing in favour of divorce, all without licences. He believed that such questions as marriage and divorce should be discussed freely without interference from the government. By this time, his wife Mary had come back to him. He was no longer interested in divorce,

Outside the law

Milton did not ask for a licence for his *Areopagitica*. He had broken the law, but he was not arrested or put on trial. He hoped that Parliament would accept his argument for press freedom, but it did not. Instead, censorship increased. Books and papers that the government did not like were banned. It was not until 1695, over 20 years after Milton's death, that his argument won and licensing was stopped. At last, books and newspapers attacking the king or the government could be printed. Today, freedom of the press is a right most countries value and people still fight to defend this right if it is threatened.

▶ John Milton spent the last years of his life quietly, writing religious poems which were licensed for printing. For the last 20 years of his life, he was blind. He spoke the words of his most famous poem, *Paradise Lost*, to his daughter and she wrote them down.

Jean Jacques Rousseau

▲ Jean Jacques Rousseau was a French writer and poet whose thoughts about politics and the freedom of the individual showed the unfairness of the government of his day. His ideas encouraged the people who wanted change to take action during and after the French Revolution of 1789.

The idea that ordinary people should have a say in how their country is governed is only about 250 years old. Before then, the most powerful people, usually the king and the richest landowners, decided what should be done. Ordinary people had to pay **taxes** to their rulers and were sent to fight for them in wartime, but they could not say how the money should be spent or whether there should be war or peace. They had to do as their rulers told them.

In France, 300 years ago, King Louis XIV was an **absolute ruler**. He alone decided how France should be run. The **peasants** who worked on the land but did not own it, paid most of the taxes. The nobles who were wealthy and did no work, paid little or no tax at all.

Jean Jacques Rousseau was a French musician and writer who worried about the unfairness of this sytem. He believed that everyone was equal and should have an equal share in government.

Inequalities

In 1762, when Rousseau was 50, he wrote a book about his ideas on government called *The Social Contract*. 'Man,' Rousseau wrote, 'though born free, is everywhere in chains.' Just as slaves wore chains, people under the rule of government had lost their freedom. A Social Contract meant an agreement between people in which they helped to protect each other's properties. It made everyone feel more secure but it meant that wealthy, powerful people ruled over the less fortunate. In this system, rulers had to be chosen to bring order into people's lives. This was not a fair government, Rousseau thought. He believed that the only good government was one that carried out the wishes of most of the people, poor as well as rich.

It was dangerous to write like this in France, and Rousseau was warned just in time, that unless he left the country he would be arrested. For the next eight years he moved around Europe, staying with

▲ Poets and philosophers gather in a Parisian drawing room in 1755. They have come to hear and discuss a new play.

Man of ideas

Thinkers die, but their ideas live on, and this is what happened to *The Social Contract* after Rousseau's death. To the French, what he wrote about ordinary people being treated like slaves seemed true. Under the rule of Louis XVI, who became King of France in 1774, life had become harder for everyone in France except for the rich and powerful. Rousseau had shown the French how life could be better and fairer for the less wealthy.

These ideas were very popular in 1789 during the French **Revolution**, when the people rose up against Louis XVI and made France into a republic. When they marched through the streets of Paris, the revolutionaries sang Rousseau's words. In other countries, too, his books were read by people who wanted to escape from the slavery of government by the rich.

friends. It was difficult to be a friend of Rousseau's. He was always arguing, and imagined that everyone was plotting against him. He returned to France for the last years of his life, becoming more and more difficult to live with. He died in 1778.

▶ The people of Paris storming a Parisian prison called the Bastille in 1789. Although Jean Jacques Rousseau had been dead for over 10 years when the French Revolution began, his ideas were still popular.

Thomas Jefferson

In the 1600s, Britain ruled 13 areas, or **colonies**, in North America. The colonies had been started by settlers from Britain. Virginia, in the south, was set up in 1607 as a trading colony. A few years later, the colonies of New England were begun by the Pilgrim Fathers from England, who wanted to be free from British rule. The British believed that the whole of North America was theirs, and that the king could give parts of it away as gifts. The colonies of Baltimore, New York and Maryland were among those which the king handed out as gifts to his family and friends.

By about 1770, the people of the colonies had come to dislike British rule. They had to pay taxes to the government in London but were not represented in the British Parliament. The British controlled the buying and selling of goods to and from the colonies.

Eventually, the colonists decided to take some action to free themselves from Britain. One of their leaders was Thomas Jefferson. In 1774, he wrote a pamphlet setting out his ideas for **independence**. Some Americans hoped that the colonies could stay British, but with more freedom to govern themselves. Jefferson believed that the colonies must become truly independent, with no ties to Britain.

The quarrel between the colonies and Britain grew quickly. In 1775, there were clashes between colonials and British troops. After more fighting the leaders decided to draw up a Declaration of Independence. Thomas Jefferson was given the job of writing the draft.

He had been well chosen for this task. Thomas Jefferson was a lawyer and landowner from Virginia. He was a learned man who had wide-ranging interests in the

◀ Thomas Jefferson, the third President of the United States from 1801 to 1809, was an important political leader and a philosopher. Two of his less well-known achievements were the passing of a law giving religious freedom to the people of Virginia and the founding of the University of Virginia in 1825.

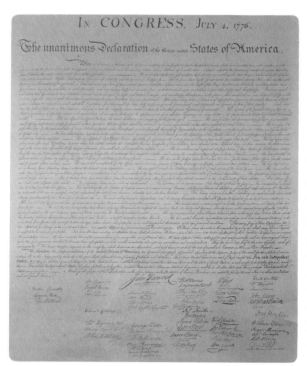

On 4 July 1776, leaders of the 13 British colonies in North America met to vote for the Declaration of Independence. The Declaration said that the people of 13 colonies had agreed to join together, with their own government, free from British rule.

President Jefferson

The American War of Independence began in 1755 and lasted for eight years. Finally in 1781 the Americans won an important victory at Yorktown in Virginia and peace was agreed. The peace treaty with the British was signed in 1783. Thomas Jefferson continued to play a leading part in government and in 1801 he became President of the United States.

▲ The Declaration of Independence, signed in 1776 by more than 50 leaders of the 13 states, is kept in the Library of Congress in Washington.

► The 13 colonies whose leaders signed the Declaration of Independence joined together in 1776 to declare themselves independent from Britain.

arts and sciences. He thought that people's talents and achievements were more important than wealth and birth.

The British had failed to provide its colonial citizens with a fair system of government, and that was why the colonies wanted to govern themselves. The Declaration explained why the colonies had decided this. All men, it said, were equal and should have the right to a free and happy life. It was the duty of governments to look after this right.

1 New Hampshire
2 New York
3 Massachusetts Bay
4 Connecticut
5 Rhode Island
6 Pennsylvania
7 New Jersey
8 Maryland
9 Delaware
10 Virginia
11 North Carolina
12 South Carolina
13 Georgia

× site of battle

NORTH AMERICA

Thomas Paine

▲ Thomas Paine was a writer who encouraged revolutionaries in America and in France to fight for freedom and equality.

There was a link between the War of Independence in the United States in 1775 and the French Revolution which broke out 14 years later. French soldiers and sailors fought for the Americans against the British, and took American ideas of freedom home with them. They had seen the Americans fight the king of England, and win.

Another European who took part in the American War of Independence was an Englishman, Thomas Paine. In 1774, he went to America to work for the revolutionary leader Benjamin Franklin. When Thomas Paine arrived there he found that people were starting to talk about independence from Britain. He wrote a pamphlet called *Common Sense* which put the argument for freedom. It sold over 100 000 copies, a huge number for those days. Paine wrote in a way that people could easily understand, and he persuaded many Americans that it was right to fight for independence. The idea that a country could be ruled without a king was one that many people, 200 years ago, could not believe. Thomas Paine's pamphlet changed their minds.

The Rights of Man

Thomas Paine returned to Britain in 1787. When revolution broke out in France in 1789, Thomas Paine and some of his friends hoped that it would spread to Britain. He believed, like Jean Jacques Rousseau and Thomas Jefferson, that everyone was equal and should be treated equally by governments. This could only happen in a republic like the United States, he said. In 1791, Paine explained his ideas in a book called *The Rights of Man*. He also wanted to help the poor with free schools, payments to help bring up children, and money for the old who could not work. Today, governments provide all these things, but 200 years ago few people believed that they should.

The Rights of Man angered and frightened the British government. The British decided to arrest Paine but he escaped to France just in time. When he arrived in Paris, the revolutionaries in France were preparing to execute King Louis XVI. Paine thought the king should be exiled, not killed. When he tried to save the king, he

▲ Thomas Paine played an important part in the early days of American independence, and was present when the leaders of the new United States signed the Declaration of Independence in July 1776.

► For the British government, the French Revolution of 1789 was an example it did not want the British people to follow. This cartoon shows Thomas Paine setting out his ideas whilst kicking away the symbols of British monarchy.

was sent to prison and was lucky to escape execution himself.

In 1802, when Paine was set free, he returned to the United States, but he quarrelled with his old friends there. He spent the last few years of his life on a farm he had been given by the state of New York. In Britain, he was not forgotten, and his ideas were taken up by others who believed in freedom and equality.

Mary Wollstonecraft

▲ Mary Wollstonecraft was a pioneer of rights for women. In her books, she pleaded for women to get a say in the running of their country, equality of education for women and employment for single women.

For many people, it was exciting to be alive at the end of the 1700s. Big changes were taking place in the way people thought and in the way they were governed. The excitement spread from the United States and France to other European countries. Thinkers began to ask all kinds of new questions. One of these was about the rights of women.

Revolutionaries in France and the United States said that all men were equal, but they said nothing about women. Very few girls went to school or had any other kind of education or training. Most women spent their lives looking after their families. If they went out to work, it was to the hardest and worst-paid jobs, usually in factories. When they married, they and anything they owned became the property of their husbands.

▼ Vasser College in the United States was the first women's college to be opened in 1861.

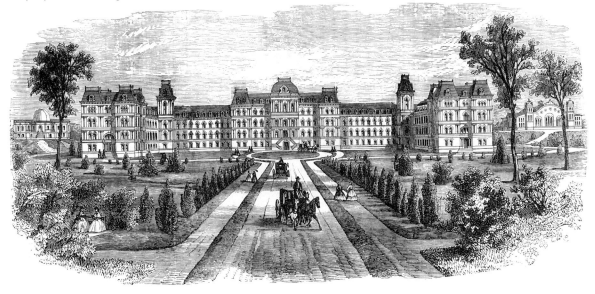

▶ Over the past 100 years, most countries have changed their laws to allow women to vote and take part in government. In 1923, Lady Astor became the first woman Member of Parliament to make a speech in the House of Commons.

The rights of women

Mary Wollstonecraft was an Englishwoman who knew how hard it was for a woman to live a life of her own. Against the wishes of her family, she left home when she was 19 to take a job as a **companion**, looking after an old woman in Bath. Later, she worked as a **governess**, teaching the children of a rich family. Companions and governesses were poorly-paid servants, but good jobs were hard to find. In 1782, she went to live with a friend, Fanny Blood, and two years later they started a school in North London. However, the school had to close down and in 1786 Mary Wollstonecraft moved to Ireland to work as a governess. The following year her first book, *Thoughts on the Education of Daughters* was published.

Although she was not badly treated by the Irish family, Mary felt that the time had come for her to live an independent life and in 1790 she moved back to London. It was there that she wrote her famous book called *A Vindication of the Rights of Women*.

Mary Wollstonecraft wrote that women were treated as if they were slaves. In fact, they had no rights. When a man died, all he owned went to his sons, and his daughters received nothing. For women, Mary said, the world was like a prison.

The fight goes on

Mary Wollstonecraft was the first woman to write about the unfair way in which women were treated. She had read Jean Jacques Rousseau's books and had liked his ideas on freedom but she disagreed with his view that women were inferior to men. After she died in 1797, other people took up her ideas. Schools and universities were opened to women. Married women won the right to own property and to end their marriages by divorce. Women could become doctors, lawyers, and work alongside men in most jobs. Although Mary Wollstonecraft died nearly 200 years ago, there are still some countries in the world today where women do not have equal rights with men.

Abraham Lincoln

▲ Abraham Lincoln was the 16th President of the United States, but the first to have been born into a poor family. During most of his time as President, the country was torn by a civil war between the northern and southern states which lasted from 1861 to 1865.

When the United States became independent, and for many years afterwards, there was one big difference between the northern states and those of the South. In the southern states, thousands of black families were kept as slaves. They could be bought and sold by their owners at will. If they escaped, they were severely beaten or even whipped to death.

Black slaves had been brought from Africa to work in the southern colonies. Thomas Jefferson had wanted to set them free, but the slave-owners argued against it. By 1850, the slavery question had split the United States. The states in the North had set their slaves free, but those in the South wanted slavery to continue. The industrial North relied on trade and shipping for its wealth whereas the South depended on farming. On the vast estates of the South, the slaves did all the work. They planted and harvested cotton and tobacco which sold for a profit in European markets.

By the 1790s the people of the United States were moving westwards, setting up new states. Some settlers wanted to work the new farms with slaves. Others wanted everyone who lived in the new states to be free. This argument had to be settled if the United States was to stay united.

Going to war

Abraham Lincoln was the son of a struggling farmer from Kentucky in the mid-west who understood the problems of the people. He wanted the new states to be places where poor families could settle and farm, and where he said 'all men would be free'. He had seen slaves working for farmers in the mid-west and he had been shocked at the sight of slaves in chains in New Orleans.

In 1860 Abraham Lincoln stood for President of the United States. He made it clear what people could expect if they voted for him. He hoped that the slavery argument could be settled peacefully, but he said it must be settled.

When Lincoln became President, the southern states broke away from the northern states of the Union. Later, the southerners formed a group of their own which they called the **Confederacy**, under their own President, Jefferson Davis of Mississippi. From then on, the two sides moved steadily towards war. In April 1861, Confederate troops attacked the Union base at Fort Sumter in South Carolina, and the Civil War began.

A shot at the theatre

By the time the war ended four years later over half a million Americans, one out of every sixty, were dead. The Union had won, and all slaves were to be freed, but great damage had been done to the United States. The South was completely shattered;

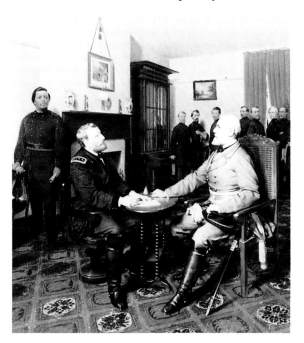

▲ A gunboat and mortar fleet bombard a fort on Island Number 10 in the Mississippi River during the Civil War. The southern troops finally surrendered after 23 days.

farms had been burnt, livestock slaughtered and cities were in ruins. Abraham Lincoln told his people that there must be no more war, and that everyone must work to 'bind up the nation's wounds'.

On 14 April 1865 Lincoln and his wife celebrated the end of the war by going to the theatre. While they were there, a gunman fired at Lincoln, wounding him so badly that he died the next day. Without his leadership, it was many years before the North and South lived easily with each other. Lincoln would be remembered for two major achievements: he had freed the slaves and held the United States together.

◀ General Lee, war leader of the southern states, surrenders to the northern leader, General Grant, at Appomattox, Virginia, in April 1865. This brought the Civil War to an end.

Karl Marx

Until about 200 years ago, most people in Europe worked on the land or in small workshops. Then the invention of new machinery brought great changes to people's lives. Factories making cloth, iron and other goods were built near large towns. People began to move to the towns from the country to find work in the new factories. However, the towns soon became overcrowded and living conditions in the cramped houses were very poor. Factory work was hard and often dangerous. People had to work long hours and were given very little time off.

Some writers thought it was wrong that people should have to live like this. One of them was a German, called Karl Marx. He believed that workers in the factories had become 'wage slaves', living only for the small amount of money they earned. Factory owners became rich, but the workers stayed poor, making money for other people.

Karl Marx studied law and philosophy, but became a writer. In his travels around Europe he met another writer, Friedrich Engels, who thought as he did. Engels had lived in England and had seen how harsh life was for cotton mill workers in Manchester. Together Marx and Engels wrote articles and books in which they said that the 'wage-slaves' should get together to take over factories from their rich owners. Marx used the word **Communism** to describe his ideas. Marx and Engels wanted a revolution.

◀ The crowded streets of Seven Dials in London show the kind of living conditions Karl Marx wanted to change. In his books, he described how workers could cooperate to improve their working lives. As members of a community, they should all be equal, he said, and be allowed to run their own country.

▲ Karl Marx was an economist and sociologist from whom the movement Marxism takes its name. His *Communist Manifesto*, written in 1848, was published on the eve of a revolution in France. Marx came to London in 1849 where he died in poverty in 1883.

A plan for revolution

In 1848, Marx and Engels wrote a pamphlet called the *Communist Manifesto* in which they described the struggle for power between two groups of people. Those who owned the land, labour and machinery and the workers who only had their labour to sell in return for wages. Marx said that power could be in the hands of the workers if they organized themselves by taking over the means of producing goods. Such revolutionary changes, Marx thought, would start in the factories and spread out until finally the workers took over the government.

Into exile

Marx's ideas got him into trouble with the governments of Belgium, France and Germany, and he was told to leave each of these countries. In 1849 he went to London, and stayed in Britain for the rest of his life. Many people were excited by Marx's revolutionary ideas and he soon became the leader of a group called the International which was formed to plan a revolution. In 1867, Marx wrote a famous book, *Das Kapital*, which showed what practical changes could be made to people's working lives and how the government would work after these changes had taken place.

Members of the International quarrelled among themselves, and the group broke up after about ten years. Marx had hoped that his ideas would bring about a fairer society, just as Jean Jacques Rousseau had done when he wrote *The Social Contract*. However, there was no revolution of the kind Marx wanted and he died in 1883, a sick and disappointed man. It was another 34 years before his ideas brought revolution in Russia, which became the first country in the world with a **Marxist** government.

▼ In this factory in Sheffield workers are making knives. People worked long hours doing a dangerous and unpleasant task without adequate protection. Marx thought that work like this took away people's dignity and made them and their managers strangers to each other.

Ch'iu Chin

◀ Women working in a Chinese silk factory in 1870. Many Chinese men thought that even this kind of work should not be done by women. Under Manchu rule, few women received any education. Ch'iu Chin was lucky to study the Greeks and to read about western history and literature.

At the time of Ch'iu Chin's birth around 1879, the Manchu family had ruled China for over 300 years. In all that time Manchu rulers had allowed very little change. The Empress Tzu Hsi had protected China from foreign influences when western traders had first entered the country. She also wished to protect traditions within Chinese families and refused to make any changes to improve people's lives, even if they were being treated unfairly.

Women in Chinese society were considered to be totally dependent on the men in their family. Chinese law said that women were not equal to men and never could be.

From a very early age all Chinese girls were taught that they had to obey their fathers until they married, then their husbands and then, if their husbands died, their sons. Women had no life of their own and had little freedom to travel around.

▶ This Chinese girl has had her feet tightly bound to keep them small. Ch'iu Chin attacked foot-binding because, she said, it helped to make women slaves.

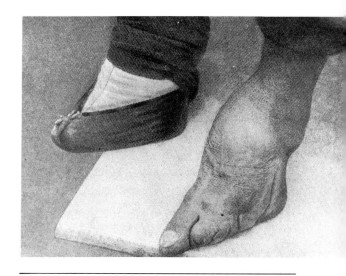

A break with the past

Ch'iu Chin's father was an official who worked for the government as a lawyer. When Ch'iu Chin was a girl, she travelled all over China with her family and saw the kind of lives that Chinese women lived. At the age of 18, she married a rich merchant, Wang T'in Chung, and they moved to Beijing. There she became involved in the opposition to the Manchu rulers. In 1904, when she was 29, she left her husband and her two children to go to study in Japan. She sold all her jewels and decided to spend her life fighting for the rights of Chinese women and for the end of Manchu rule.

Many other people who wanted a revolution in China had moved to Japan to be able to fight in safety. When Ch'iu Chin arrived in Japan, she joined a group of revolutionaries and she stayed in Japan for two years. She wanted to show that women could behave as they pleased and so she learned riding and sword-fighting. She often dressed in western-style clothes. While she was in Japan she wrote a set of songs called *Stones of the Jingwei Bird*.

Ch'iu Chin chose to write songs because this was a way of spreading her ideas to ordinary Chinese women. Few of them could read or write, but they sang songs as they worked, which they had learnt by heart. Ch'iu Chin's songs were about how the Chinese could free themselves from Manchu rule, and how Chinese women could escape being ruled by men.

Back to China

In 1906, Ch'iu Chin went back to China to carry on her work there. In the girls' school where she taught, she told her students about some of the famous women of history, such as Boudicca and Joan of Arc. She encouraged her students to become independent and above all to become educated. When Ch'iu Chin was not teaching she went on helping to plan a revolution to get rid of the Manchus. At the same time, she began a newspaper for women and started a women's army.

Ch'iu Chin's ideas were becoming dangerous to the Manchus, and in 1907 she was arrested and executed. Although she had failed to overthrow the Manchus, when the Chinese Revolution came four years later, women helped to end the rule of the Manchus for ever. After the revolution was over, a special meeting was held to remember the part Ch'iu Chin had played in preparing women for it. Today her achievements as a pioneer for women's rights, her role in the revolution of China and her writings as a poet are all recognized.

31

Franklin D Roosevelt

In 1930 the world was hit by a terrible **depression**. The economic changes that took place after the First World War had upset the balance of world trade. On 21 October 1929 a serious financial crisis known as the 'Wall Street Crash' hit the American stock market and affected the whole nation.

The United States had prospered by trading with the rest of the world but in the 1930s few countries could afford to buy American goods. Farmers could not sell the food they had grown, and factories could not sell the goods they had made. Many firms went out of business and so millions of people became unemployed. One out of every four Americans was out of work. Many people who had lent money to banks and businesses lost it all. There seemed to be no hope for anyone.

In 1932, a new President of the United States was elected. His name was Franklin Delano Roosevelt. He believed that if the United States made a big effort it could solve its problems. He had had to fight against a big problem in his own life. Ten years before becoming President, he had caught polio, a serious illness that left him unable to use his legs. This did not stop him working, or presenting himself for President.

Speaking to the people

Roosevelt saw that the most important task was to let the Americans see that there was a way out of the depression. They must not give up hope. 'We have nothing to fear,' he told them, 'but fear itself.' As soon as Roosevelt became President, he began what

▲ On 12 March 1933, President Roosevelt became the first leader to use radio to talk to the people to explain emergency measures during the depression. He continued to keep people informed and in a speech before Congress in January 1941, he outlined the 'Four Freedoms' which he said people would enjoy after the war. These were freedom of speech, freedom of worship, freedom from want and freedom from fear.

he called the New Deal. This was a whole programme to help people create work. It provided jobs building roads, bridges, harbours and airports and it helped to get trade started again. Old crowded houses were pulled down and new ones were built to replace them. The United States Congress approved the lending of money to people who still could not find work. There were tax cuts for farmers and people were encouraged to return their savings to the banks.

President Roosevelt changed the way that the United States government worked. Before, it had tried to find reasons for doing things. He looked for ways of getting things done. Slowly, life in the United States began to improve. There was more work, and people had more money to spend. Roosevelt was elected President for another four years, in 1932, 1936, 1940 and 1944.

At war

Soon, Roosevelt had to face another problem. In Europe, the Second World War had started in 1939. The Germans invaded France in 1940 and Britain had been attacked by German bombers. Some Americans wanted the United States to stay out of the war, but Roosevelt wanted to help Britain defend itself. The war, he said, was a fight for freedom against slavery. Roosevelt ordered financial help for Britain. When the United States joined the war in 1941, Roosevelt and the British leader, Winston Churchill, worked together to win it. They signed an agreement to help each other. American ships crossed the Atlantic Ocean with food and supplies for the **Allies** who were fighting Hitler, the German leader.

Roosevelt did not live to see the end of the Second World War. Less than a month before Germany surrendered on 12 April 1945, he died suddenly. He had been an important statesman who had helped his country out of the depression and acted as a major ally during the war. In helping the Allies, Roosevelt had put an end to the American policy of 'isolation' which had prevented the United States from getting involved in other countries' problems.

▼ The Watts Bar Dam in Tennessee. The dam was built in 1933 under the New Deal programme.

▼ Franklin D Roosevelt (centre), Winston Churchill (left) and Joseph Stalin (right) met in 1945 to discuss the war against Germany.

George Orwell

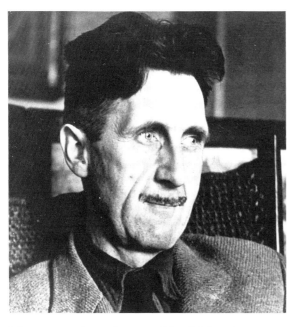

Animal Farm

George Orwell wanted to explain his thoughts on what had happened in Russia in a way that people could understand easily. He had the idea of telling a story based on the Russian Revolution as if it were about animals rather than people. Orwell called his book *Animal Farm*.

The farm in the story is run by a farmer who is so cruel that the animals meet and decide to run the farm by themselves. The pigs are the leaders of the animal revolution, and at first it seems as if things are going well. Then, bit by bit, the pigs begin to behave as cruelly as the farmer. They tell the other animals that they must work much harder. One hard-working horse, Boxer, wears himself out and the pigs quietly send him away to be killed. Life gets worse for the animals that are left, until the pigs have become absolute rulers, giving the others orders. At the end of the book the pigs are practising walking on two legs, like people. The other animals are as unhappy and as badly treated as they were before the revolution.

Orwell meant his readers to see that the story of the farm was based on the Russian Revolution and its betrayal of the people it promised to help. The pigs represented Stalin and his friends, and the other animals represented ordinary people.

Many people in Europe liked Marx's Communist ideas and hoped that they would spread. George Orwell, an English writer, was not a Communist but he had also written about the injustices which the less fortunate people in society suffered when rulers misused their power.

The first people in the world to have a government based on Karl Marx's ideas were the Russians. In 1917, there was a revolution in Russia and a group of workers called the Bolsheviks took over the government. At the head of the group was Lenin, the revolutionary leader. In the struggle for power that followed, a new leader, Joseph Stalin, was elected. During his rule, Stalin enforced a brutal system of peasant reforms and took away people's freedoms. Life in Russia under Stalin was no better than it had been before the Revolution.

▲ This is Napoleon the pig in the cartoon film of *Animal Farm*, which was made in 1954.

▼ In 1936, there was war in Spain between the politically left-wing 'Popular Front' and the government of the political right. Orwell went there to report on the war. In Barcelona, he fought against the Communists and was forced to flee in fear of his life. In *Homage to Catalonia*, he gives an account of his Spanish experiences and his dread of Communism.

Orwell's nightmare

As Orwell grew older, he felt that the threat of being ruled by a brutal government was becoming a reality for more people all over the world. He came to believe that no government in any country really cared about the lives of ordinary people. He felt that whether a country was ruled by a king, a president or a Communist leader, the rulers were only interested in themselves. New inventions, he thought, could be used by rulers to harm people. One day, governments would invent devices to find out what people were thinking, and punish them if they had revolutionary ideas. A year before he died he wrote another story which he called *1984*. The book gave a vivid picture of the unjust and all-powerful government he feared would make people become the slaves of their rulers. Like *1984*, *Animal Farm* was a warning of what could happen if people let any government have too much power.

Winston Churchill

THE BRITISH COMMONWEALTH OF NATIONS

TOGETHER

◄ This poster appeared all over Britain in 1940. It urged the British people to work together to win the war.

In May 1940, people in Britain stayed close to their radios to hear the latest news about the development of the Second World War. Hitler, the German leader, had planned to regain the lands Germany had lost after the First World War. In 1938, he took control of Austria, then Czechoslavakia. When Hitler invaded Poland in September 1939, Britain and France declared war on Germany.

By April 1940, the war had been going for seven months, but there had been little fighting. Suddenly, German troops began to move forward across western Europe. They invaded Denmark and Norway and then Holland, Belgium, Luxembourg and France. By the end of May, Allied troops had to be withdrawn from Dunkirk, and France was lost to Hitler. Britain was now in danger of being invaded, too. The British Parliament met to discuss the crisis.

They decided that the Prime Minister, Neville Chamberlain, had failed to secure peace with Hitler and must leave the government. In his place, they chose Winston Churchill.

'We will never surrender'

Churchill was 66 years old. He had been in Parliament for 40 years and a government minister for part of that time. In the 1930s, when Adolf Hitler became leader of Germany, Churchill had warned Britain that there would be war, but no one had listened. Before the war began, he had called for a stronger army, navy and air force to match Germany's, but by the beginning of the war Britain's forces were still weak. He had been proved right.

In 1940, Churchill became Prime Minister of a country in crisis. His first task was to

◀ Winston Churchill knew how important it was to make himself known to everyone. His cigar and his 'V for victory' sign were seen everywhere.

Churchill's leadership

There were two reasons why Churchill was such an important war leader. He had read and written a great deal of history. He understood how government worked and why men like Hitler wanted to rule the world. He also knew how to communicate his unshakeable belief that Britain would win the Second World War.

After 1945, the British had had enough of war. They chose a different government for peacetime, though Churchill later became Prime Minister again from 1951 to 1955. When he died in 1965, aged 95, leaders from all over the world came to London to remember the leader who had helped save the world from rule by Adolf Hitler.

encourage the British people to fight by every means, 'by sea, land and air'. He used the radio to speak to the people. He told them that the war was going to be long and hard, but that Britain would win in the end. If the Germans landed in Britain, he said, they would have to fight for every street. More tanks, guns, ships and aircraft were needed quickly. Churchill met President Roosevelt and asked for help from the United States. 'Give us the tools,' he told the Americans, 'and we will finish the job'. At home, Churchill persuaded the British to throw all their effort into making weapons.

It was two years before Britain began to win the war, with the help of the United States and the other Allies. There were many set-backs before Hitler died and Germany accepted defeat. At last, in 1945, there was peace.

▼ Britain stopped work for the day of Churchill's funeral in 1965. The cranes of London's docks were dipped as a salute to a great leader.

Bertrand Russell

Some people believe that it is always wrong for a country to go to war. They are called **pacifists**. They believe that war brings nothing but unhappiness to people, and that what people want most in the world is to live in peace.

Bertrand Russell was a pacifist and a clever scholar, studying mathematics and philosophy. He believed that the rules of mathematics could be used as a guide to all thinking. In 1910, he became a lecturer at Cambridge University.

Four years later, the First World War started between Britain and Germany. Bertrand Russell spoke out against the war and was punished for doing so. He was fined £100, sent to prison for six months and dismissed from his job in Cambridge. In spite of all this, he went on saying that the war was wrong.

Looking into the future

As a pacifist, Bertrand Russell supported Prime Minister Chamberlain's efforts in 1938 to get a peace agreement from Hitler. Russell disliked the Second World War as much as the First World War, but he agreed that it was necessary to defeat Hitler in order to secure a lasting peace.

Over the next 15 years, Bertrand Russell **campaigned** tirelessly by appearing on television, writing books and giving speeches to convey his peace message to the world. When the **atomic bomb** was tested in 1945, Bertrand Russell spoke against it in a famous radio broadcast called 'Man's Peril'.

Banning the bomb

Bertrand Russell's work on mathematics and philosophy made him famous all over the world, but his views on war made him disliked by the British government. In Britain, a group called The Campaign for Nuclear Disarmament (CND) was formed in 1958 to call for Britain and America to give up their atomic weapons. Bertrand Russell became one of CND's leaders. Two years later, he left CND to form a more active group of protesters called the Committee of 100. The campaigners' aim was to encourage other people to protest

▼ Bertrand Russell at Cambridge University in 1945. He had just finished his *History of Western Philosophy*, which told the story of thinkers from Socrates to the present day.

► Bertrand Russell and his third wife in their garden at Cambridge. During his life, he travelled to China and the Soviet Union in 1920 and he toured the United States as a lecturer during 1938 and 1939. It was on his return to Britain in 1944 that he took up a post as lecturer and fellow at Cambridge University.

actively by marching through the streets. As far as the police were concerned, this was an offence called 'a breach of the peace' which was punishable by prison sentence or a fine. For a short time, when he was an old man of 89, Bertrand Russell was put in prison.

Bertrand Russell spent the last years of his life as a world leader of people who wanted peace. When he died, aged 98, he still believed that a third World War could break out at any time. The peace movements Bertrand Russell started have continued to work actively for peace and many more people have been inspired by his actions.

► The CND peace movement took part in 'sit-down protests' against the use of atomic weapons, when they sat outside public buildings in London and refused to move. Bertrand Russell took part in many sit-down protests in the 1960s.

A S Neill

Many great thinkers have had ideas about how children can best be taught so that they grow up happily. Jean Jacques Rousseau was one, but his own children had a very unhappy time. Bertrand Russell started a school, but it was a failure. A S Neill was Scottish schoolteacher who was able to make his own ideas work. His school, Summerhill, became famous all over the world.

Neill was born in 1883. His father was head of a village school in Scotland. Schools were very different in those days. No talking was allowed. Children were beaten with the strap if they did the slightest thing wrong or did not understand lessons they were taught. Neill hated school, and he hated it even more when he became a teacher himself. He decided that there had to be a better way of teaching and learning.

◄ A S Neill died in 1973 but his daughter, Zoe, continues his work at Summerhill where she is the head.

Life at Summerhill

Neill dreamed of starting a school of his own where he could carry out his own ideas. In 1921, he helped to open the International school in Germany, which later moved to Austria and then England. However, he was not happy until he had opened his own school. Three years later he achieved this ambition by opening a school in Britain which he called Summerhill. The school moved from one place to another over the years, but the name stayed the same.

Neill wanted to let children take part in the running of the school. Most teachers at that time thought that children were 'bad', and teaching must make them 'good'. Neill argued that children were good to start with, but poor teaching made them 'bad'. At Summerhill, children learned because the teachers made lessons interesting and fun. No one said that the children had to go to lessons, but they did because they wanted to. Neill did not believe in competition, so there were no team games against other schools and no one was judged to be top or bottom of the class. Boys and girls were taught together which was unusual at that time in Britain. Summerhill welcomed children who were unhappy and had behaved badly in other schools. Neill had been unhappy as a child and felt he could help these children. 'I am on the same side as the child,' he said.

▲ All the children and teachers at Summerhill had a weekly meeting, where they agreed on school rules that would be best for everyone. Neill often spoke, but it was the children who decided what to do.

Summerhill USA

Some of the parents who sent their children to Summerhill were Americans who were living in Britain, and they helped to spread Neill's ideas to the United States. His book about Summerhill was published there in 1960, and some American teachers started schools like Neill's. The book was also studied in universities where teachers were trained.

In Britain too, some of Neill's ideas were copied by teachers in ordinary schools. Now, there is much more freedom and fun in schools than there used to be, and teachers and children are more friendly. All children at school, not just those at Summerhill, have a better time because of Neill's views on education.

▼ Neill did not care much how he or the Summerhill children dressed. He believed that comfortable clothes were the best for teaching and learning.

Nelson Mandela

South Africa is a country where the population is divided by race, under a system called **apartheid**, or separateness. Under apartheid white and black people lead separate lives. However, black people in South Africa are not treated on an equal basis with white people. The whites own most of the land and its wealth of crops and minerals, and make the laws of the country.

The original white settlers were Dutch. They arrived in South Africa in 1652, at about the same time as the black Nguni tribes, who had migrated south down through Africa. The Dutch colonists fought the Nguni tribes and established themselves. By 1913, the former Dutch colonies in South Africa had been given independence, and 88 per cent of the land was given to white settlers.

A hard life

For more than 70 years after this blacks were restricted by the laws made by the white people, and the living conditions of most blacks were bad. Black people had to work for the whites, as the land left for blacks to live on was too poor to support them. Often, black people had to go to the cities to find work. Blacks were allowed to live in areas called 'townships', close to the white cities but could not buy houses in white areas. The laws of apartheid allowed only the whites to live and work where they chose, while black people needed permission from the government to travel around. Black people who did not have permission, in the form of a permit or 'pass',

were often arrested and imprisoned when they moved into white areas to find work.

The ANC

These bad social conditions meant that many organisations were formed to fight for better living and working conditions for black people. One was the African National Congress, or ANC. Among the men who joined the ANC was a young black lawyer, Nelson Mandela. He proved to be an excellent leader, and in 1950 became president of the ANC's Youth League.

The ANC adopted a policy of peaceful protest against apartheid, and conducted a very popular campaign of defiance against the white government during 1952. In 1955

▼ The young Nelson Mandela was arrested in 1952 during the ANC's peaceful defiance campaign against the South African government. The ANC was fighting for better living and working conditions for black people.

the ANC published its famous 'Freedom Charter', which gives basic human rights to all people in South Africa. The Freedom Charter was designed to show the world how hurtful apartheid was, especially for black people.

The protests of the ANC were met with fierce police action, and in 1960 police fired on a crowd of people demonstrating peacefully against the pass laws in Sharpeville. 69 people were killed and 180 injured. Soon afterwards the South African government banned the ANC.

The Congress began to meet in secret, and Nelson Mandela became the leader of a group which planned to resist the government by a campaign of **sabotage** — that is, destroying government property. Nelson also visited Europe and many African states seeking support for the fight against apartheid.

Mandela goes to prison

In 1962 Nelson Mandela and seven other activists were arrested at a farmhouse in Rivonia, Johannesburg. The famous Rivonia trial followed, where Nelson used his legal skills to defend himself and to argue passionately for freedom for all the black people of South Africa. Nelson and his

fellow activists were sentenced to life imprisonment for attempted sabotage, however.

Nelson Mandela became the world's most famous prisoner. He was imprisoned on a bleak island called Robben Island, near Cape Town. While he was in prison he studied for more degrees and encouraged his fellow prisoners to improve themselves by study and discipline. He and the other prisoners had many serious discussions about politics and about the future of South Africa.

Nelson's second wife, Winnie, was very supportive. She made speeches and wrote books reminding people why her husband was imprisoned and what life was like for black people in South Africa.

Hope for the future

Nelson's influence inside and outside South Africa grew so great that the governments of the world eventually forced the South Africans to release him. In February 1990 Nelson Mandela was released from prison and allowed to take up his political work again. By this time the South African government had begun to end the policy of apartheid, and the man who had been imprisoned as a terrorist was now able to take part in planning South Africa's future.

▶ Nelson Mandela was arrested in 1962 for plotting to blow up government property. Two years later he was sent to prison for life. He spent 27 years in prison and was finally released on 11 February 1990.

Time chart

Date	Europe, Australia, New Zealand	Asia	Africa	North, Central and South America
BC				
450	Socrates and Plato in Athens			
342	Aristotle becomes tutor to Alexander the Great			
336	Aristotle returns to Athens and opens the Lyceum			
AD				
1265	Thomas Aquinas begins writing *The Sum of Theology*			
1302	Dante Alighieri goes into exile and begins writing *The Divine Comedy*			
1509	Desiderius Erasmus writes *In Praise of Folly*			
1518	Erasmus begins translating the *New Testament* into Latin			
1609	Galileo Galilei designs his telescope			
1632	Galileo publishes a book proving Copernicus' theory that the Sun is the centre of the solar system			
1633	Galileo faces trial by the Inquisition			
1644	John Milton writes *Areopagitica*			
1762	Jean Jacques Rousseau writes *The Social Contract*			
1775-1783				The American War of Independence
1776				The United States Declaration of Independence
1789	The French Revolution			
1790	Mary Wollstonecraft writes *A Vindication of the Rights of Women*			
1791	Thomas Paine writes *The Rights of Man*			
1800				Thomas Jefferson becomes third President of the United States
1848	Marx and Engels write the *Communist Manifesto*			
1860				Abraham Lincoln is elected President of the United States
1861-1865				The American Civil War
1867	Karl Marx writes *Das Kapital*			

Date	Europe, Australia, New Zealand	Asia	Africa	North, Central and South America
1904		Ch'iu Chin travels to Japan to lead her new revolutionary life		
1911		The Chinese Revolution begins		
1914-1918	——————————————— The First World War ———————————————			
1917	The Russian Revolution			
1924	A S Neill opens Summerhill School			
1932				Franklin D Roosevelt becomes President of the United States
1936-1945	The Spanish Civil War			
1939-1945	——————————————— The Second World War ———————————————			
1940	Winston Churchill becomes Prime Minister of Britain			
1941		Japan attacks the United States Navy at Pearl Harbour and brings the United States into the Second World War		
1945	George Orwell's *Animal Farm* and Bertrand Russell's *A History of Western Philosophy* are published			
1949	George Orwell's *1984* is published			
1960			South African police kill 69 Blacks at Sharpeville	
1962			Nelson Mandela is arrested	
1964			Nelson Mandela is sentenced to life imprisonment	
1990			Release of Nelson Mandela	

Glossary

absolute ruler: a person who has complete control over a country, or part of a country, and all the people in it. Absolute rulers include kings, queens, emperors, sultans, tsars and dictators

Allies: the name given to the group of countries including Australia, New Zealand, France, Belgium and the United States which supported Britain against Germany during the Second World War

apartheid: the government-controlled system in South Africa which separates black people from white people

astronomy: the study of the stars and planets and other objects in space

atomic bomb: a type of bomb that works by splitting the atom, causing a huge explosion. An atom is the smallest part of any substance

ban: to refuse to allow people to express their opinions on a subject by forbidding all writings, speeches and actions which refer to that subject

biology: the scientific study of animals and plants

campaign: to work hard to bring the public's attention to a particular opinion or problem

censorship: the action of making alterations to a piece of writing or stopping it being published

civilization: a group of people who have settled in one place to live. They have rules and laws about the way they live and behave

colony: territory in one country ruled from another country

communicate: to pass ideas and information on to other people by means of speech, writing or in some other way

Communism: a political belief that all members of the community should be treated equally. Communists believe that a country should be run by its workers rather than by its rulers

companion: a servant who lives with and looks after an old or sick person

Confederacy: the group of southern states which broke away from the northern states of the Union during the American Civil War

debate: a discussion where several people put forward their differing ideas and opinions

depression: a period of hardship and unemployment. A depression may be caused by a country if it produces too many goods which it finds it cannot sell because they are too costly for people to buy

exile: to live away from one's own country, either by choice or as a result of being forced to leave

governess: a woman servant of a wealthy family who is employed to teach young children

independence: the freedom to make decisions and take actions without having to ask permission from another person or country

Inquisition: the court of the Catholic Church which tried people it suspected of breaking the laws of the Church. The word inquisition means an investigation or inquiry into something

licence: written permission from a government which allows a person to do something

Marxist: a person who believes in the ideas of Karl Marx

pacifist: a person who believes that war is always wrong and refuses to take part in any kind of warfare

peasant: a person who works on the land for very poor wages

philosophy: the study of the writings of thinkers who search for the truth about human existence

politics: the way that a community or country is organised and run and the study of how governments work

Protestant: the part of the Christian Church which does not accept the Pope as its leader

reason: the use of thought to answer problems and form opinions

republic: a country or part of a country which is ruled by its people through their chosen representatives

revolution: a complete and sudden change in the way a country is governed when the people of that country overthrow their ruler or government

sabotage: the destruction of something as a means of protest

satire: a form of humour which ridicules a person or a government as a way of criticising them

scholar: a person who spends time studying and learning

tax: a payment which the people of a country must make to their government. Taxes pay for the running of the government and all the services that it provides

theology: the study of religion

Index